CATHOLIC
CHRISTMAS
PRAYERS

Catholic Christmas Prayers

BY MARIE NOËL

ADAPTED & COMPILED FROM
APPROVED SOURCES

BOOKSBYNOËL.COM

Catholic Christmas Prayers

ISBN-13: 978-0-9837887-4-4

Interior design & typesetting: Renata L. Reyez
Cover image: "The Nativity" (circa 1508 - 1519)
by Juan de Flandes, courtesy National Gallery of
Art, Washington, D.C.

BooksByNoël.com

First Edition

Contents

Dedication

I dedicate this work to my niece who has a special love for the Christ Child. Since her earliest years, she has loved the Baby Jesus. As an adult, she continues to hold this devotion dear to her heart as she has worked and cared for children with special needs. She and these children share a special bond which I think is rooted in her great love for the innocent Baby Jesus born in Bethlehem.

The photos of the Christ Child are images from her collection of Baby Jesus statues. This statue of St. Anthony and the Child Jesus is her favorite.

Introduction

As Christmas approached, I began thinking about how much Jesus is missing from Christmas. I've noticed in a personal way since my name is Noël as well as from my point of view as a Catholic.

Since my youth, I've always looked forward to this one time in the year when I could find a coffee mug, an ornament, a Christmas card or other small token with my name on it. It's been getting harder and harder every year until it's now practically impossible to find anything at all. Santas, snowmen, snowflakes, and reindeer abound as the commonplace symbols for Christmas rather than Christ. Most of us know about the ample efforts to remove the Christian significance of Christmas in our society.

Yet, Christmas began with Christ. He is the reason for it. In the Catholic faith, we acknowledge him at this holy time of year. Also, we honor the Nativity, as we call it, as well as his Incarnation. The book contains various prayers, mostly from the 1800s. The prayers focus on preparing for Christ's coming at Christmas, His Infancy, and the Epiphany.

I hope these prayers enhance your spiritual life. May the Christ Child bless you abundantly as I wish you a very Merry Christmas!

Chapter 1

ADVENT

CHRISTMAS WITHOUT CHRIST

How can I keep my Christmas feast
In its due festive show,
Reft of the sight of the High Priest
From whom its glories flow?
I hear the tuneful bells around,
The blessed towers I see:
A stranger on a foreign ground,
They peal a fast for me.
O Britons! now so brave and high,
How will ye weep the day
When Christ in judgment passes by,
And calls the Bride away!
Your Christmas then will lose its mirth,
Your Easter lose its bloom:
Abroad, a scene of strife and dearth;
Within, a cheerless home!

(Blessed John Henry Newman)
– Dec. 25, 1832

Origin of Advent

Advent is a time of fasting, penance, meditation and prayer established by the Catholic Church. It is meant to prepare us to celebrate the feast of Christmas.

It starts on the Sunday near the feast of St. Andrew and ends on Christmas Eve. It consists of four Sundays that signify the 4,000-year waiting for the coming of Jesus.

The earliest records of Advent being observed date back to the year 380 in a canon council at Saragossa.

To Mary

O God, who were pleased that your Word should take flesh, at the message of an Angel, in the womb of the Blessed Virgin Mary: grant to your suppliants, that we who believe her to be truly the mother of God, may be helped by her intercession. *Amen.*

Any Time
During Advent

Stir up, O Lord, your power, and come and mercifully fulfill that which you promised to your Church unto the end of the world.

Stir up, we ask you, O Lord, our hearts to prepare the ways of your only-begotten Son; that by his Advent we may be enabled to serve you with purified minds; through the same Jesus Christ our Lord.

We ask you, O Lord, to purify our consciences by your daily visitation; that when your Son our Lord comes he may find in us a mansion prepared for himself; through the same Jesus Christ our Lord.

Make us, we ask you, O Lord our

God, watchful and alert in awaiting the coming of your Son Christ our Lord that when he shall come and knock, he may find us not sleeping in sins, but awake, and rejoicing in his praises; through the same Jesus Christ our Lord.

We ask you, Almighty God, let our souls enjoy this their desire, to be inspired by your Spirit; that being filled, as lamps, by the divine gift, we may shine like blazing lights before the presence of your Son Christ at his coming; through the same Jesus Christ our Lord.

We ask you, O Lord our God, let us all rejoice with upright hearts, being gathered together in the unity of faith; that at the coming of your Son our Savior, we may go unstained to meet him, in the company of his saints; through the same Jesus Christ our Lord.

We ask you, Almighty God, to hear our prayers, and to pour out upon us your loving tenderness; that we who are afflicted by our sins may be refreshed by the Advent of our Savior; through the same Jesus Christ our Lord.

We ask you, O Lord our God, to strengthen our minds by your divine power; that at the coming of our Lord Jesus Christ your Son, we may be found worthy of the banquet of eternal life; through the same Jesus Christ our Lord.

Grant, we ask you, Almighty God, this grace for your people, to wait with all vigilance for the coming of your only-begotten Son; that as he, the author of our salvation, taught us, we may prepare our souls like blazing lamps to meet him, through the same Jesus Christ our Lord.

Incline, O Lord, your merciful ears to our voice, and illuminate the darkness of our hearts by the light of your visitation. Who lives and reigns with the Father and the Holy Ghost, one God, world without end.

Make us, O Lord, to detest our own evils with our whole heart; that at the coming of your Son our Lord, we may receive his good things, through the same Jesus Christ our Lord.

Mercifully hear, O Lord, the prayers of your people; that as they rejoice in the Advent of your only-begotten Son according to the flesh, so when he comes a second time in his majesty, they may receive the reward of eternal life; through the same Jesus Christ our Lord.

Grant we ask you, Almighty God, that the coming solemnity of our redemption may both provide us help in this present life, and also enrich us with the bliss of life eternal; through Jesus Christ our Lord.

Be you to us, O Lord, a crown of glory in the day when you shall come to judge the world by fire; that you may clothe us here with the robe of righteousness, and hereafter with the perfection of a glorious liberty; through your mercy.

Come to deliver us, O Lord God of hosts; turn us again, and show your face, and we shall be saved; so that being cleansed by your mercy with the gift of worthy repentance, we may be enabled to stand before you in the judgment; through your mercy.

O Christ our God, who will come to judge the world in the manhood you assumed, we pray you to sanctify us completely, that in the day of your coming, our whole spirit, soul, and body may so have a fresh life in you, that we may live and reign with you forever.

O Lord God, Father Almighty, purify the secrets of our hearts, and mercifully wash out all the stains of sin; and grant, O Lord, that being cleansed from our crimes by the benediction of your tenderness, we may without any terror await the fearful and terrible coming of Jesus Christ our Lord.

O God, who didst look on man

when he had fallen down into death, and resolve to redeem him by the Advent of your only-begotten Son; grant, we ask you that they who confess his glorious incarnation may also be admitted to the friendship of him, their Redeemer; through the same Jesus Christ our Lord.

O wisdom that came from the mouth of the most high, reaching from one end to another, mightily and sweetly ordering all things; come to teach us the way of understanding.

O Adonai, and Leader of the house of Israel, who did appear to Moses in the flame of the burning bush, and gave the law on Sinai; come to deliver us with an outstretched arm.

O root of Jesse, who stands as a

sign to the people; before whom kings shall shut their mouths, who nations shall ask; come to deliver us now, delay not.

O key of David, and scepter of the house of Israel, who opens and no man shuts, and shuts and no man opens, come and bring forth the prisoner out of the prison-house, where he sits in darkness and the shadow of death.

O day-spring, splendor of the eternal light, and sun of righteousness; come and enlighten those who sit in darkness and the shadow of death.

O king of Gentiles, you who they long for, and cornerstone that makes both one; come and save man whom you formed out of the clay.

O Emmanuel, our king and lawgiver, the expected one of the Gentiles, and their Savior; come to save us, O Lord our God. *Amen.*

Short Weekly Prayers

1st Week

Raise up our hearts, O Lord, we ask you, in expectation of the coming of your only Son: that, by his advent, being reconciled to you, we may serve you in holiness all the days of our lives. *Amen.*

2nd Week

Stir up our hearts, O Lord, to prepare the ways of your only-begotten Son that by his coming we may be worthy to serve you with purified minds. Grant this through our Lord Jesus Christ, your Son, who lives and reigns with you and the Holy Spirit one God, forever and ever. *Amen.*

3rd Week

We ask you, O Lord, lend your ear to our prayers and enlighten the darkness of our mind, by the grace of your visitation. Grant this through our Lord Jesus Christ, your Son, who lives and reigns with you and the Holy Spirit one God, forever and ever. *Amen.*

4th Week

Stir up your might, we ask you, O Lord. Come and help us with your great power that with the help of your grace, your mercy may accelerate the goodness that our sins impede. Grant this through our Lord Jesus Christ, your Son, who lives and reigns with you and the Holy Spirit one God, forever and ever. *Amen.*

Other Weekly Prayers

1st Sunday

Arouse, O Lord, we ask you by your power to come. That from the dangers which threaten, we may merit to be rescued by you our protector; saved by you our liberator. Who lives and reigns with God, the Father, in the unity of the Holy Ghost, God, world without end.

O God, who willed that your Word should, at the message of an angel, take flesh in the womb of the Blessed Virgin Mary; grant to us who believe her to be truly the mother of God that we may be aided by her intercession with you. *Amen.*

2nd Sunday

Stir up our hearts, O Lord to prepare the ways of your only-begotten Son; that with minds purified by his advent, we may be worthy to serve you. Who lives and reigns with you and the Holy Spirit one God, forever and ever.

Arouse, O Lord, we ask you by your power to come. That from the dangers which threaten, we may merit to be rescued by you our protector; saved by you our liberator. Who lives and reigns with God, the Father, in the unity of the Holy Ghost, God, world without end.

O God, who willed that your Word should, at the message of an angel, take flesh in the womb of the Blessed Virgin Mary; grant to us who believe her to be truly the mother of God that we may be aided by her intercession with you. *Amen.*

3rd Sunday

Incline your ear, O Lord we ask you, to hear our prayers and enlighten the darkness of our mind by the grace of your visitation. Who lives and reigns with God, the Father, in the unity of the Holy Ghost, God, world without end.

Arouse, O Lord, we ask you by your power to come. That from the dangers which threaten, we may merit to be rescued by you our protector; saved by you our liberator. Who lives and reigns with God, the Father, in the unity of the Holy Ghost, God, world without end.

O God, who willed that your Word should, at the message of an angel, take flesh in the womb of the Blessed Virgin Mary; grant to us who believe her to be truly the mother of God that we may be aided by her intercession with you. *Amen.*

4th Sunday

Arouse your might, we ask you,

O Lord, and come and help us with great power, that by the aid of your grace, your mercy will hasten what our sins obstruct. Who lives and reigns with you and the Holy Spirit one God, forever and ever.

Arouse, O Lord, we ask you by your power to come. That from the dangers which threaten, we may merit to be rescued by you our protector; saved by you our liberator. Who lives and reigns with God, the Father, in the unity of the Holy Ghost, God, world without end.

O God, who willed that your Word should, at the message of an angel, take flesh in the womb of the Blessed Virgin Mary; grant to us who believe her to be truly the mother of God that we may be aided by her intercession with you. *Amen.*

*"Madonna and Child with St. Jerome,
St. Bernardino, and Angels" by Sano di Pietro
(1460-1470). Courtesy National Gallery of
Art, Washington, D.C.*

Chapter 2

TO THE CHRIST CHILD

The Child laid in a lowly manger: this is God's sign. The centuries and the millennia pass, but the sign remains, and it remains valid for us too – the men and women of the third millennium.

It is a sign of hope for the whole human family; a sign of peace for those suffering from conflicts of every kind; a sign of freedom for the poor and oppressed; a sign of mercy for those caught up in the vicious circle of sin; a sign of love and consolation for those who feel lonely and abandoned. A small and fragile sign, a humble and quiet sign, but one filled with the power of God who out of love became man.

(Blessed John Paul II)
– Dec. 24, 2002

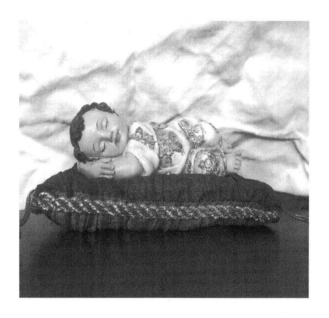

To Jesus as an Infant

I give you thanks, most loving Jesus, because you chose to hide the glories of your divinity, and for our sake to become a little child, to be born in a poor stable of a poor mother, to be wrapped in poor clothes, and to be laid in a manger.

Grant, dearest Jesus, that I may be like you, humble and poor in spirit; and as you were obedient to your mother, the holy Virgin Mary, and to your foster-father, the blessed St. Joseph, so I may be ever obedient to my earthly parents, for your sake, who are my heavenly father and shepherd; that as I grow in age, I may also grow day by day in wisdom and holiness; and as you,

O my Savior, you chose while on earth to live in poverty, so I may ever honor and love the poor, to treat them kindly, and to share with them whatever I may have. Give me, O Jesus, a mild, humble, loving, and compassionate spirit toward all men, striving in all things to imitate your most perfect example. Hear this my prayer, O most merciful Savior, I humbly ask you. Amen.

*"The Flight into Egypt" by Vittore Carpaccio
(circa 1515). Courtesy National Gallery of
Art, Washington, D.C.*

Mysteries of the Holy Infancy

- *Incline unto my aid, O God.*

- *O Lord, make haste to help me.*

- *Glory be to the Father, and to the Son, and to the Holy Ghost. As it was in the beginning, is now, and ever shall be, world without end. Amen.*

- *Our Father, who art in heaven, hallowed be thy name, thy kingdom come, thy will be done, on earth as it is in heaven. Give us this day our daily bread, and forgive us our trespasses, as we forgive those who trespass against us. And lead us not into temptation, but deliver us from evil. Amen.*

1. The Incarnation

Jesus, sweetest child, who, coming down from the bosom of the Father for our salvation into the womb of the Virgin Mary, where, conceived by the Holy Ghost, you, the Word Incarnate, took the form of a servant. Have mercy on us.

- *Have mercy on us, Child Jesus. Have mercy on us.*

- *Hail Mary, full of Grace, the Lord is with thee: blessed art thou among women, and blessed is the fruit of thy womb, Jesus. Holy Mary, mother of God, pray for us sinners, now and at the hour of our death. Amen.*

2. The Visitation

Jesus, sweetest child, who, by your Virgin Mother, visited St. Elizabeth, and filled your precursor, John the Baptist, with the Holy Ghost, sanctifying him from his mother's womb. Have mercy on us.

- *Have mercy on us, Child Jesus. Have mercy on us.*
- *Hail Mary...*

3. The Expectation of the Birth

Jesus, sweetest child, who, for nine months hidden in your mother's womb, and awaited for the time of your birth and, in the meantime, inflamed the heart of the Virgin Mary and by St. Joseph, was by them offered to God the Father for the salvation of the world. Have mercy on us.

- *Have mercy on us, Child Jesus. Have mercy on us.*
- *Hail Mary...*

4. The Holy Nativity

Jesus, sweetest child, born in Bethlehem of the Virgin Mary, wrapped in swaddling clothes, laid in the manger, glorified by angels, visited by shepherds. Have mercy on us.

- *Have mercy on us, Child Jesus. Have mercy on us.*

- *Hail Mary...*

O Jesus, born of virgin bright, infinite glory be to you. Praise to the Father infinite, and Holy Ghost eternally.

5. Christ Is At Hand

Come, let us adore him.

- *Our Father...*

6. The Circumcision

Jesus, sweetest child, circumcised when eight days old and called by the glorious name of Jesus, and, proclaimed by your name and by your blood, to be the Savior of the world. Have mercy on us.

- *Have mercy on us, Child Jesus. Have mercy on us.*

- *Hail Mary...*

"The Presentation in the Temple" by Augustin Hirschvogel (1549). Courtesy National Gallery of Art, Washington, D.C.

7. Adoration of the Kings

Jesus, sweetest child, made known to the three Magi by a star, adored on Mary's bosom, honored with the mystical gifts of gold, frankincense, and myrrh. Have mercy on us.

• *Have mercy on us, Child Jesus. Have mercy on us.*

- *Hail Mary…*

8. The Presentation

Jesus, sweetest child, presented in the temple by the Virgin Mary. Jesus, embraced by the holy old man Simeon, and revealed to the Jews by Anna the prophetess. Have mercy on us.

- *Have mercy on us, Child Jesus. Have mercy on us.*

- *Hail Mary…*

9. The Flight into Egypt

Jesus, sweetest child, who Herod sought to slay, carried by St. Joseph with your mother into Egypt, saved from a cruel death by flight, and glorified by the blood of the holy Innocents. Have mercy on us.

- *Have mercy on us, Child Jesus. Have*

mercy on us.

- *Hail Mary...*

O Jesus, born of virgin bright, infinite glory be to you. Praise to the Father infinite, and Holy Ghost eternally.

Christ is at hand. Come, let us adore him.

- *Our Father...*

10. The Stay in Egypt

Jesus, sweetest child, who, with Mary most holy, and the patriarch St. Joseph, lived in exile in Egypt for seven years, where you uttered your first words, and left your swaddling clothes, first began to walk upon this earth, and in the destruction of the idols, did work in a hidden manner your first miracles. Have mercy on us.

- *Have mercy on us, Child Jesus. Have mercy on us.*

- *Hail Mary...*

11. The Return from Egypt

Jesus, sweetest child, who when Herod was dead, was recalled out of Egypt into the land of Israel, and in journey suffered many hardships while carried back by Mary and

St. Joseph to the city of Nazareth. Have mercy on us.

• *Have mercy on us, Child Jesus. Have mercy on us.*

• *Hail Mary...*

12. The Life in the Holy House

Jesus, sweetest child, who in the holy of Nazareth lived most holy and passed your life in obedience, poverty, and work. As you grew in years, you showed to God and men signs of wisdom and grace. Have mercy on us.

• *Have mercy on us, Child Jesus. Have mercy on us.*

• *Hail Mary...*

13. The Disputing with the Doctors

Jesus, sweetest child, brought to Jerusalem when 12 years old, was lost by your parents, and sought for by them with sorrow, and after 3 days was found to their great joy, with the doctors in the temple. Have mercy on us.

- *Have mercy on us, Child Jesus. Have mercy on us.*

- *Hail Mary...*

O Jesus, born of virgin bright, infinite glory be to you. Praise to the Father infinite, and Holy Ghost eternally.

- *Our Father.*

Christ is at hand.

Come, let us adore him.

Let Us Pray

Almighty and everlasting God, Lord of heaven and earth, who revealed yourself to little ones, grant, we ask you, that while we celebrate and honor the most holy mysteries of your Son, the Child Jesus, and strive to imitate them, we may arrive at that heavenly kingdom which you promised to little children, through the same Jesus Christ our Lord, who lives and reigns with you and the Holy Spirit one God, forever and ever. *Amen.*

Litany of the Infant Jesus

Lord have mercy on us. *Christ have mercy on us.*

Lord have mercy on us. *Christ hear us. Christ graciously hear us.*

God the Father of heaven. *Have mercy on us.*

God the Son, Redeemer of the world. *Have mercy on us.*

God the Holy Ghost. *Have mercy on us.*

Holy Trinity, one God. *Have mercy on us.*

Infant Jesus Christ. *Have mercy on us.*

Infant, true God. *Have mercy on us.*

Infant, Son of the living God. *Have mercy on us.*

Infant, Son of the Virgin Mary. *Have*

mercy on us.

Infant, begotten before the daystar.
Have mercy on us.

Infant, the Word made flesh. *Have mercy on us.*

Infant, the wisdom of your Father.
Have mercy on us.

Infant, the integrity of your Mother.
Have mercy on us.

Infant, the only-begotten of your Father. *Have mercy on us.*

Infant, the first born of your Mother.
Have mercy on us.

Infant, the image of your Father.
Have mercy on us.

Infant, the origin of your Mother.
Have mercy on us.

Infant, the brightness of your Father.
Have mercy on us.

Infant, the honor of your Mother.

Have mercy on us.

Infant, equal to your Father. *Have mercy on us.*

Infant, subject to your Mother. *Have mercy on us.*

Infant, the delight of your Father. *Have mercy on us.*

Infant, the riches of your Mother. *Have mercy on us.*

Infant, the gift of your Father. *Have mercy on us.*

Infant, the treasure of your Mother. *Have mercy on us.*

Infant, the creator of man. *Have mercy on us.*

Infant, the fruit of a Virgin. *Have mercy on us.*

Infant, the virtue of God. *Have mercy on us.*

Infant, the companion of man. *Have*

mercy on us.

Infant, our God. *Have mercy on us.*

Infant, our brother. *Have mercy on us.*

Infant, pilgrim on earth, yet in the fruition of glory. *Have mercy on us.*

Infant, possessed of heavenly bliss, yet in the pilgrimage of mortality. *Have mercy on us.*

Infant, a perfect man from your Mother's womb. *Have mercy on us.*

Infant, endowed with the wisdom of old age from your childhood. *Have mercy on us.*

Infant, the Father of ages. *Have mercy on us.*

Infant, of a few days. *Have mercy on us.*

Infant, life in want of food. *Have mercy on us.*

Infant, the Word reduced to silence. *Have mercy on us.*

Infant, crying in the crib. *Have mercy on us.*

Infant, thundering in heaven. *Have mercy on us.*

Infant, the terror of hell. *Have mercy on us.*

Infant, the joy of paradise. *Have mercy on us.*

Infant, formidable to tyrants. *Have mercy on us.*

Infant, desired by the wise men. *Have mercy on us.*

Infant, exiled from your people. *Have mercy on us.*

Infant, king in your exile. *Have mercy on us.*

Infant, the over thrower of idols. *Have mercy on us.*

Infant, zealous for your Father's glory. *Have mercy on us.*

Infant, strong in your weakness. *Have mercy on us.*

Infant, powerful in your littleness. *Have mercy on us.*

Infant, treasure of grace. *Have mercy on us.*

Infant, light of glory. *Have mercy on us.*

Infant, fountain of love. *Have mercy on us.*

Infant, source of sanctity. *Have mercy on us.*

Infant, the restorer of lost heaven. *Have mercy on us.*

Infant, the repairer of the earth. *Have mercy on us.*

Infant, the head of Angels. *Have mercy on us.*

Infant, the root of patriarchs. *Have mercy on us.*

Infant, the word of the prophets. *Have mercy on us.*

Infant, the desire of nations. *Have mercy on us.*

Infant, the joy of the shepherds. *Have mercy on us.*

Infant, the light of the sages. *Have mercy on us.*

Infant, the salvation of the infants.
Have mercy on us.

Infant, the expectation of the just.
Have mercy on us.

Infant, the teacher of the wise. *Have mercy on us.*

Infant, the first fruit of all saints. *Have mercy on us.*

Be merciful; spare us, Infant Jesus. *Be merciful; hear us, Infant Jesus.*

From the yoke of slavery weighing on the children of Adam. *Infant Jesus, deliver us.*

From the captivity of the devil. *Infant Jesus, deliver us.*

From the wickedness of the world. *Infant Jesus, deliver us.*

From the concupiscence of the flesh. *Infant Jesus, deliver us.*

From the pride of life. *Infant Jesus, deliver us.*

From inordinate curiosity. *Infant Jesus, deliver us.*

From blindness of mind. *Infant Jesus, deliver us.*

From a perverse will. *Infant Jesus, deliver us.*

From our sins. *Infant Jesus, deliver us.*

Through your most pure conception. *Infant Jesus, deliver us.*

Through your most humble birth. *Infant Jesus, deliver us.*

Through your tears. *Infant Jesus, deliver us.*

Through your most painful circumcision. *Infant Jesus, deliver us.*

Through your most glorious manifestation. *Infant Jesus, deliver us.*

Through your most devout presentation. *Infant Jesus, deliver us.*

Through your most innocent

conversation. *Infant Jesus, deliver us.*

Through your most divine life. *Infant Jesus, deliver us.*

Through your poverty. *Infant Jesus, deliver us.*

Through your sufferings. *Infant Jesus, deliver us.*

Through your travels and labors. *Infant Jesus, deliver us.*

Lamb of God, who takes away the sins of the world. *Infant Jesus, deliver us.*

Spare us, O Infant Jesus.

Lamb of God, who takes away the sins of the world. *Hear us, O Infant Jesus.*

Lamb of God, who takes away the sins of the world. *Have mercy on us, O Infant Jesus.*

Jesus Infant. *Hear us.*

Jesus Infant. *Graciously hear us.*

Let Us Pray

O Lord Jesus! O Lord Christ, you were pleased so to humble yourself in your incarnate divinity and most sacred humanity as to be born in time and become a little child. Grant that we may acknowledge infinite wisdom in the silence of a child, power in weakness, and majesty in humiliation. Adoring your humiliations on earth, may we contemplate your glories in heaven, who with the Father and the Holy Spirit, lives and reigns forever.

May the Infant Jesus Christ hear us, now, and forever. *Amen.*

"*The Nativity*" *by Lorenzo Lotto (1523).*
Courtesy National Gallery of Art, Washington, D.C.

Chapter 3

SPECIAL CHRISTMAS PRAYERS

Long awaited, the splendor of the new Day at last shines forth. The Messiah is born, Emmanuel, God-with-us! He is born, who was announced by the Prophets of old and long invoked by all "who dwelt in the land of gloom". In the silence and the darkness of the night, the light becomes a word and message of hope. But does this certainty of faith not seem to clash with the way things are today?

If we listen to the relentless news headlines, these words of light and hope may seem like words from a dream. But that is precisely the challenge of faith, which makes this proclamation at once comforting and demanding. It make us feel that we are wrapped in the tender love of God, while at the same time it commits us to a practical love of God and of our neighbor.

(Blessed John Paul II)
– Dec. 24, 2001

*"The Nativity" by Giuliano Traballesi
(1727-1812). Courtesy National Gallery
of Art, Washington, D.C.*

At Midnight on Christmas Eve

O God, who has made this most sacred night shine forth with the brightness of the true light, grant, we ask you, that having known the mystery of his light on earth, we may partake of His joys in heaven. Amen.

Litany for Christmas

Glory be to God on high. *And peace on earth to men of goodwill.*

We praise you. *We bless you.*

We adore you. *We glorify you. We give you thanks for your great glory.*

Lord God, heavenly king, Father Almighty. *Lord Jesus Christ, the only-begotten Son.*

Lord God, Lamb of God, Son of the Father, who takes away the sins of the world. *Have mercy on us.*

Who takes away the sins of the world. *Hear our prayers.*

Who sits at the right hand of the Father. *Have mercy on us.*

For you only are holy. You only are our Lord. You only, O Jesus Christ, are most high, together with the Holy Ghost, in the glory of God the Father.

Blessed Jesus, true God and man, born in the form of a helpless infant. *Praise and glory be to you forever.*

Blessed Jesus, who, having the heavens for your throne, yet chose a poor stable for your abode. *Praise and glory be to you forever.*

Blessed Jesus, who, being God incomprehensible, in love for us was wrapped in swaddling clothes, and laid in a manger. *Praise and glory be to you forever.*

Blessed be the Lord God of Israel, because he has visited and has brought the redemption of his people.

• *And he has raised up to us a powerful salvation in the family of David his servant.*

As he spoke by the mouth of his holy Prophets, who were from the beginning.

•   *That he would save us from our enemies, and from the hand of all that hate us.*

To show his mercy towards our fathers, and to be mindful of his holy covenant.

•   *According to the oath which he swore to our father Abraham to grant us.*

That, being delivered from the hands of our enemies, we might serve him without fear.

•   *In holiness and justice before him all our days.*

Through the depths of the mercy of our God, the rising light has visited us from on high.

•   *To enlighten those that sit in darkness, and in the shades of death, to direct our feet in the way of peace.*

• *Glory be to the Father and to the Son and to the Holy Spirit. As it was in the beginning is now, and ever shall be, world without end. Amen.*

Let Us Pray

O eternal God, Father Almighty, who in compassion to lost mankind sent your only Son to become our Redeemer from that unhappy state, grant, we ask you, that we, who acknowledge the mercy of this time, may find the benefit of it in our souls, in the pardon of all our sins Grant this through our Lord Jesus Christ, your Son, who lives and reigns with you and the Holy Spirit one God, forever and ever. *Amen.*

On Christmas Eve

O God, who made us glad with the yearly expectation of our redemption, grant that as we joyfully receive your only-begotten Son as our Redeemer, we may also see him without fear when he comes as our judge; even our Lord, who with you lives and reigns with you and the Holy Spirit, one God, forever and ever.

Grant, O merciful God, that for the reception of the transcendent mystery of your Son's nativity, the minds of believers may be prepared, and also the hearts of unbelievers subdued; through the same Jesus Christ our Lord who lives and reigns with you and the Holy Spirit, one God, forever and ever.

O God, who made this most sacred night to shine with the illumination of the true light; grant, we ask you, that as we have known the mystery of that light upon earth, we may also perfectly enjoy it in heaven; through the same Jesus Christ our Lord who lives and reigns with you and the Holy Spirit, one God, forever and ever. *Amen.*

"The Nativity" by Ludwig Krug (1516).
Courtesy National Gallery of Art, Washington,
D.C.

At Day Break

Grant, we ask you, Almighty God, that as we are bathed in the new light of your incarnate Word, what shines in our minds by faith, may be resplendent in our works. Through our Lord Jesus Christ, your Son, who lives and reigns with you and the Holy Spirit one God, forever and ever. *Amen.*

On Christmas Day

Grant, we ask you, Almighty God, that the new birth in the flesh of your only-begotten Son may deliver us, whom the ancient bondage holds under the yoke of sin. Through our Lord Jesus Christ, your Son, who lives and reigns with you and the Holy Spirit one God, forever and ever. *Amen.*

Another

for

Christmas Day

Grant us, we ask you, O Almighty God, that we, who are filled with the new light of your Incarnate Word, may show in our works what faith displays in our minds. Grant this through our Lord Jesus Christ, your Son, who lives and reigns with you and the Holy Spirit one God, forever and ever. *Amen.*

Christmas Day Thanksgiving

"A child is born to us, a Son is given to us, whose empire is upon his shoulder."(Isaiah, ix. 6.)

What thanks, O Lord, shall we give to you for such a benefit!

A noble family is naturally glad at the birth of an heir to its wealth and dignity, and why should not we offer you "a host of praise," since, outcasts as we were, the universal heir is given to us, who like to us in all things, except in sin, will raise up our fallen hopes, and restore us to the glorious liberty of children of God.

O admirable, O counselor, O strong, O Father of the future age! O Prince of peace!

May your angels praise you, and may the just bless you for this immense condescension forever and ever. *Amen.*

• *Praise the Lord, all you nations, praise him, all you people.*

• *Because his mercy is confirmed on us and his truth remains forever.*

*"The Nativity with the Annunciation to
the Shepherds" by Master of the Dominican
Effigies (circa 1340). Courtesy National
Gallery of Art, Washington, D.C.*

Christmas Day Petitions

Grant O merciful God, that He who was born this day to be the Savior of the world, as he is the author of our divine birth, so may be himself the giver of our immortality; through Jesus Christ our Lord who lives and reigns with you and the Holy Spirit, one God, forever and ever.

Almighty and everlasting God, who willed that on the nativity of our Lord Jesus Christ, your Son, should depend the beginning and the completion of all religion; grant us, we ask you, to be seen as one part of him, on who is built the whole

salvation of mankind; who with you
lives and reigns with you and the
Holy Spirit, one God, forever and
ever.

We ask you, O Lord, grant to
your servants the increase of faith,
hope, and charity; that as they glory
in the birth of your Son our Lord,
they may, by your governance, not
feel the adversities of this world;
and also that what they desire to
celebrate in time, they may enjoy
to all eternity; through Jesus Christ
our Lord who lives and reigns with
you and the Holy Spirit, one God,
forever and ever.

O God, who are pleased to save,
by the nativity of your Christ, the
race of man, which was mortally
wounded; grant, we ask you, that

we may not cling to the source of our perdition, but be transferred to the fellowship of our Redeemer; who with you lives and reigns with you and the Holy Spirit, one God, forever and ever.

Grant we ask you, O Lord our God, that we who rejoice to keep the feast of the nativity of Jesus Christ our Lord, may by joining him gain his friendship, through Jesus Christ our Lord who lives and reigns with you and the Holy Spirit, one God, forever and ever.

Grant, O Lord, we ask you, to your people a strong firmness of faith; that as they confess your only-begotten Son, the everlasting partaker of your glory, to have been born in our very flesh, of the Virgin Mother, they may be delivered from present struggles, and admitted into joys that shall abide; through Jesus Christ our Lord who lives and reigns with you and the Holy Spirit, one God, forever and ever.

Grant we ask you, O Lord our God, that your church may apprehend both parts of the one mystery, and adore one Christ, both God and man, neither divided from our nature nor separate from your essence; through Jesus Christ our Lord who lives and reigns with you and the Holy Spirit, one God, forever and ever.

Grant we ask you, Almighty God, that the new birth of your only-begotten Son in the flesh may set free those bound by sin; through Jesus Christ our Lord who lives and reigns with you and the Holy Spirit, one God, forever and ever.

Grant we ask you, O our God, that your family, which has been saved by the nativity of your Son our Lord Jesus Christ, may also quietly rest with him as the perpetual Redeemer, who with you and the Holy Spirit, one God, forever and ever.

Almighty and everlasting God, who by your only-begotten Son made us to be a new creation for yourself, preserve the works of your mercy, and cleanse us from all our ancient stains; that by the assistance of your grace we may be found in his form, in whom our substance dwells with you, through Jesus Christ our Lord who with you and the Holy Spirit, one God, forever and ever.

Be present, O Lord, to our prayers; and let your people, who were formed by you and restored by your power, be also saved by your continual help, through Jesus Christ our Lord who lives and reigns with you and the Holy Spirit, one God, forever and ever.

Grant we ask you, Almighty God, that as we are bathed in the new light of your Incarnate Word that shines by faith in our minds may enlighten our actions; through Jesus Christ our Lord who lives and reigns with you and the Holy Spirit, one God, forever and ever.

Grant to us, Almighty God, that as your salvation, wondrous with a new and heavenly light, went forth on this day to redeem the world, so it may ever beam forth in the renewal of our hearts; through Jesus Christ our Lord who lives and reigns with you and the Holy Spirit, one God, forever and ever.

Merciful and most loving God, by whose will and generosity Jesus Christ our Lord humbled himself for this—that he might exalt the whole race of man; and descended to the depths for the purpose of lifting up the lowly; and was born, God-Man, by the Virgin, for this reason—that he restore in man the lost heavenly image; grant that your people may stay with you, that as you redeemed them through your goodness, they may always please you by devoted service.

Blessed be the Lord God, who comes in the name of the Lord, and whose coming has redeemed us, whose birth has enlightened us; who by his coming has found the lost, and illuminated those who sat in darkness. Grant, therefore, O Father Almighty, that we celebrating with devotion the day of his birth, may find the day of judgment a day of mercy; that as we have known his kindness as our Redeemer, we may feel his gentle tenderness as our judge.

We give you thanks, O Lord our God, and bless you from day to day, who brought us to this your holy day. Give us, with your faithful people, peace and quietness through many succeeding years to welcome this your birthday, through your mercy.

Almighty and everlasting God, who has made holy this day by the incarnation of your Word, and the child-bearing of the Blessed Virgin

Mary; grant your people a share in this celebration, that they who have been redeemed by your grace may be happy as your adopted children; through Jesus Christ our Lord who lives and reigns with you and the Holy Spirit, one God, forever and ever.

Almighty and everlasting God, the light of the faithful and the ruler of souls, who has blessed us by the incarnation of your Word, and the child-bearing of the Blessed Virgin Mary; we ask you, let the power of your Holy Spirit come also upon us, and the mercy of the highest overshadow us.

O Christ, Almighty Son of God, come graciously on the day of your nativity to be the Savior of your people; that with your goodness you may deliver us from all anxiety and all earthly fear, who lives and reigns with you and the Holy Spirit, one God, forever and ever.

We ask you, O Lord, let our hearts be graciously enlightened by the holy radiance of your Son's incarnation; that so we may escape the darkness of this world, and by his guidance arrive at the country of eternal brightness; through Jesus Christ our Lord who lives and reigns with you and the Holy Spirit, one God, forever and ever.

O God who made the most glorious name of our Lord Jesus Christ, your only-begotten Son, to be sweet and lovable to your faithful servants, and tremendous and terrible to evil spirits; mercifully grant that all who devoutly honor this name of Jesus

on earth, may in this life receive the sweetness of holy comfort, and in the life to come the joy of gladness and never-ending jubilation; who lives and reigns with you and the Holy Spirit, one God, forever and ever. *Amen*

*"Adoration of the Magi" by Giovanni Battista
Castello (1547-1637). Courtesy the Walters
Art Museum.*

Chapter 4

NOVENAS

The message of Christmas makes us recognize the darkness of a closed world, and thereby no doubt illustrates a reality that we see daily. Yet it also tells us that God does not allow himself to be shut out. He finds a space, even if it means entering through the stable; there are people who see his light and pass it on. Through the word of the Gospel, the angel also speaks to us, and in the sacred liturgy the light of the Redeemer enters our lives.

Whether we are shepherds or "wise men" – the light and its message call us to set out, to leave the narrow circle of our desires and interests, to go out to meet the Lord and worship him. We worship him by opening the world to truth, to good, to Christ, to the service of those who are marginalized and in whom he awaits us.

(Pope Benedict XVI)
– Dec. 25, 2007

"*Madonna and Child with the Infant St. John*"
by an artist after Correggio (circa 1510).
Courtesy National Gallery of Art, Washington,
D.C.

Christmas Novena

Hail, and blessed be the hour and moment at which the Son of God was born of a most pure Virgin at a stable at midnight in Bethlehem. In the piercing cold at that hour vouchsafe, I ask you, to hear my prayers and grant my desires (mention your request here). Amen.

Novena to the Child Jesus

(To Prepare for Christmas Day, Dec. 16 to Dec. 24)

1. Eternal Father, I offer to your honor and glory, and for my own

salvation, and for the salvation of the whole world, the mystery of the birth of our Divine Savior.

• *Glory be to the Father and to the Son and to the Holy Spirit. As it was in the beginning is now, and ever shall be, world without end. Amen.*

2. Eternal Father, I offer to your honor and glory, and for my eternal salvation, the sufferings of the most Holy Virgin and of St. Joseph in that long and weary journey from Nazareth to Bethlehem. I offer you the sorrows of their hearts when they found no place to shelter themselves, when the Savior of the world was to be born.

• *Glory be...*

3. Eternal Father, I offer to your honor and glory, and for my eternal

salvation, the sufferings of Jesus in the stable where he was born, the cold he suffered, the swaddling clothes that bound him, the tears he shed, and his tender infant cries.

- *Glory be...*

4. Eternal Father, I offer to your honor and glory, and for my eternal salvation, the pain that the holy Child Jesus felt in his tender body when he submitted to circumcision. I offer you that precious blood which then, for the first time, he shed for the salvation of the whole human race.

- *Glory be...*

5. Eternal Father, I offer to your honor and glory, and for my eternal salvation, the humility, mortification, patience, charity, all the virtues of the Child Jesus; and I thank you, and I

love you, and I bless you without end, for the mystery of the Incarnation of the divine Word.

- *Glory be...*

- *The Word was made flesh.*

- *And dwelt amongst.*

Let Us Pray

O God, whose only-begotten Son was made manifest to us in the substance of our flesh, grant, we ask you, that through him, whom we acknowledge to be like unto ourselves, our souls may be inwardly renewed. Who lives and reigns with you forever and ever. *Amen.*

Novena to Jesus for the New Year

(Dec. 23 to Dec. 31)

Oh most sweet Infant Jesus, who at the end of eight days did submit to be circumcised, receiving the holy name of Jesus, and becoming, in virtue of that name and by the shedding of that blood, the Savior of the world, I humble myself before you, and thank you with all my heart for this your great mercy and love to me and to all poor sinners. The sight of this your blood reminds me hopefully of the source from where flows every grace, every grace that will be given to me during the year; and also of the place where I will seek shelter and help in every trouble. It is your heart, dear Lord, which was opened to me in this first shedding of your blood.

Therefore I devote to you, oh sweetest, dearest heart, every word and deed, every beat of my heart, all that I do or suffer during this year. Accept my offering, and strengthen me with your grace; enlighten and shield me, and grant me in virtue of your name, that most holy, most efficacious name of Jesus, this is my request. Hear me, oh Jesus, for the sake of this your name and of your loving heart. *Amen.*

*"The Adoration of the Magi" by Giovanni di
Paolo (circa 1450). Courtesy National Gallery
of Art, Washington, D.C.*

Novena for the

Feast of the Epiphany

(Dec. 28 to Jan. 5)

I salute you O divine heart, with the three Magi who offered their homage to you.

Look on me, I ask you, with the same love and kindness with which you received them, that I may offer with my heart, gold, frankincense and myrrh; that is to say, my intellect, my memory and my will, completely to you, in faith, hope, charity, in thought, word and deed.

Accept my offering, accept my heart, and grant that I may live and die thanking you for the invaluable favor of being called to the true faith.

Therefore, I ask of you, by the joy which filled your heart, when you did see the first of the Gentiles at your feet, to hear my prayer and grant the request I make in this novena. *Amen.*

Novena

in Honor of the

Name of Jesus

O merciful Jesus, in early infancy began as our Savior, by shedding your precious blood, and assuming for us that name which is above all names; we thank you for such early proofs of your infinite love; we venerate your sacred name, in union with the profound respect of the angel who first announced it to the earth, and unite our affections to the sentiments of tender devotion, which the adorable name of Jesus has, in all ages, enkindled in the hearts of your servants.

Animated with a firm faith in your unerring word, and penetrated with confidence in your mercy, we now most humbly remind you of the promise you made, that, when two or three should gather in your name, you yourself would be among them. Come, then, among us, most amiable Jesus, for it is in your sacred name we are here assembled.

Come into our hearts, that your Holy Spirit may pray in and by us; and mercifully grant us, through that adorable name, which is the joy of heaven, the terror of hell, the consolation of the afflicted, and the solid ground of our unlimited confidence, all the petitions we make in this Novena.

O blessed Mother of our Redeemer, who participated so sensibly in the sufferings of your dear Son, when he shed his sacred blood, and assumed for us the name of Jesus; obtain for us, through that adorable name, the favors we ask in this Novena.

Beg also, that the most ardent love may imprint on our hearts that sacred name Jesus, that it may be always in our minds, and on our lips; that it may be our defense in temptations, and our refuge in danger during our lives; and our consolation and support in the hour of death. *Amen.*

Chapter 5

OTHER PRAYERS

Today Christmas has become a commercial celebration, whose bright lights hide the mystery of God's humility, which in turn calls us to humility and simplicity. Let us ask the Lord to help us see through the superficial glitter of this season, and to discover behind it the child in the stable in Bethlehem, so as to find true joy and true light.

(Pope Benedict XVI)
– Dec. 24, 2011

For the Church

Mercifully hear, O Lord, we ask you, the prayers of your Church; that all adversities and errors being destroyed, she may serve you with secure liberty. Amen.

For the Pope

O God, the pastor and ruler of all the faithful, look favorably on your servant ____, whom you have set as pastor over your Church; grant, we ask you, that both by word and example he may edify those over whom he is placed, so that with the flock committed to his care, he may attain everlasting life. Through our Lord Jesus Christ, your Son, who lives and reigns with you and the Holy Spirit one God, forever and ever. *Amen.*

To the Virgin Mary

O God, who through the Virgin Mary, has given mankind the rewards of eternal salvation grant, we ask you that we may experience her intercession for us, by whom we have been found worthy to receive the author of life, our Lord Jesus

Christ. Grant this through our Lord Jesus Christ, your Son, who lives and reigns with you and the Holy Spirit one God, forever and ever. *Amen.*

Other Prayers to the Blessed Virgin Mary

O Mary, Virgin Mother of the Messiah, help me, by your prayers, to love him as you did, that is, with my whole strength: and lead me to Bethlehem, of which you are queen. You holy Angels, help me to stand near in your glorious choir, near the crib of our God; help me with your heavenly influence, to share in your adorations, and, under the shadow of your sacred wings, to hide my spiritual poverty.

All you saints of God, by the delights you found in the mystery of Bethlehem, help me; and be near me, now that the great God, who filled you with light and love, is about to come into the poor dark dwelling of my heart.

Mary, Mother of my Jesus, pray for me, that this gracious visit of your divine Son may produce in me abundant fruits of virtue.

You holy angels of God, who adore him now dwelling within me, be solicitous for the holiness and purity of my soul and body.

All you saints of God, pray for me,

that I may always be faithful to him,
whom you loved on earth, and now
love eternally in heaven. *Amen.*

A Prayer in Remembrance of the Manger Crib

I adore you, Incarnate Word, true
Son of God from all eternity, and
true Son of the Virgin Mary in the
fullness of time! Adoring your divine
person, and the humanity that is
united to it, I feel moved, to honor
the poor crib which welcomed you,
an infant, and was truly the first

throne of your love. Would that I could prostrate myself before it with the simplicity of the shepherds, with the faith of Joseph, with the love of Mary! Would that I could bend in adoration of so precious a memorial of our salvation, with the spirit of mortification, of poverty, of humility, with which you, the Lord of heaven and of earth, chose a manger to receive and shelter your trembling limbs!

Will you, O Lord, who, while yet a babe, rested in this crib, also to pour into my heart a little of the joy that was excited by those who saw your lovely childhood, and the wonders which accompanied your birth; through which I ask you to give to the whole world peace and good will, and, in the name of all

mankind, to give all thanks and glory to the Father, and to the Holy Ghost, who, with you, lives and reigns, one God, world without end. *Amen.*

*"The Nativity with Six Dominican Monks"
by Master of Imola (1265-1274). Courtesy
National Gallery of Art, Washington, D.C.*

Prayer of Thanks for Virtuous Women who Helped in the Coming of the Messiah

I thank you, O Lord my God, for having inspired so many virtuous women to do what they have done to prepare the way for the Messiah in the world and in hearts, as well as for the zeal with which women in our own times have labored to keep alive the sacred fire of the sanctuary, while all conspired to extinguish it. May their example be forever imitated, through the same Jesus Christ our Lord.

- *Drop down dew, ye heavens, from*

above, and, ye clouds, rain down the just one.

•   *Let the earth open and bud forth a Savior.*

O Lord, who from the beginning was promised to be our Redeemer and our Savior, moved by your mercy, and touched by our sinfulness, exert your power and come to save us, that, by your assistance, and our faith in you, we may escape the evils without number which threaten us, who lives and reigns with God the Father, in the unity of the Holy Ghost, one God, world without end. *Amen.*

Before Communion

Act of Faith

You are about to descend, O eternal God, and yet, there is nothing to indicate your approach. As on the sacred night of your birth, your entrance into Bethlehem was in humility and in silence; so also now, there is nothing to tell that you are about to visit me. A little child, veiled under the appearance of a humble host, is coming to me, and, in a few moments, I shall hold within me him who created all things, the judge of the living and the dead! Oh how I love to bow down my reason before this wonderful mystery!

How I love, too, to contemplate this humility of my God, to which he has humbled himself in order that he might exalt me. No, reason could never have taught me all this. How could reason tell me what the infinite love of God for his creatures can do, when I cannot even make me see my own nothingness and sinfulness, into which, you, dear Jesus, are now coming? O infant God!

I believe in your love, and your love is limitless. I come to you with a simple faith, as the shepherds went to Bethlehem when the angel spoke these words to them: There is born unto you, in the city of David, a Savior, who is Christ the Lord: and this shall be a sign unto you: — you shall find the infant wrapped in swaddling-clothes, and laid in a crib. They went without delay, and found you, and believed. I would do likewise, O my Savior! The sacramental veils which cover you, are to me, what your infancy, your swaddling clothes and your crib, were to them; and I believe you are here really present. Accept this my firm faith, and receive me as one of those humble shepherds, whose simplicity merited for them the first place at the feast of Bethlehem. *Amen.*

Act of Humility

But, sweet Savior, these shepherds of Bethlehem had another offering besides the simplicity of their faith, which made them pleasing to you.

It was the humility of their hearts.

You love the humble, O my God, and therefore you preferred these humble men to all the rest of mankind, giving them the grand honor of being the first worshippers at your crib. The humility of Mary drew you from heaven into her chaste womb; and the humility of these fortunate herdsmen made you call them to be the first to form, with Mary, Joseph, and the angels, your court in this humble stable, which your adorable presence converted into a paradise.

In this you gave an important lesson to me, who am to be favored as they were and about to receive you within myself. Spare me not, my beloved Jesus; lower my prideful spirit; destroy the conceited ambitions of my heart; cast me down at the foot of your crib, and let me not to rise again, until I have become one of those little children, whom you so loved, that you would be one; so the better to come down even so low as to me.

It is as a weak baby that you come to me, O infinite God! What can I do, but sink into my nothingness. In your divine humility, you wouldn't be born in any other place than a stable and a crib; my heart, then, will satisfy you, dear Jesus, and Bethlehem itself, compared with me, had not a poverty so worthy of that majesty, which loves to descend to what is lowest, and of that light which glories in shining where the darkness is thickest. *Amen.*

*"The Nativity" by Fra Filippo Lippi and
Workshop (circa 1445). Courtesy National
Gallery of Art, Washington, D.C.*

Act of Adoration

You have, then, come down even unto me, O my sovereign Lord and are resting in my heart, as in a crib, which you have chosen for yourself, O infant God. My heart is now become like a new Bethlehem, O bread of angels.

I most devoutly adore you the great God thus humbling yourself to such lowliness. To the hymn of the angels, Glory be to God in the highest; I must add, Glory be to you, my God, in this depth of my misery and weakness, where you have so mercifully come.

Who will teach me, my sweetest infant guest? Who will teach me how to give you a worthy welcome of homage?

Mary, your most pure and Blessed Mother, you were born placed you in the crib, humbled herself before you as your humble handmaid, and adored you. Permit me to imitate your beloved Mother, and adore you as she did, O my Lord! I humbly ask you to accept her homage to supply for the unworthiness of mine: for, she is my Mother, and you willed that all her riches and merits should belong to her children.

I offer you, likewise, the adorations of that just man, the chaste spouse of Mary, the admirable Joseph, who shared in the divine secret of Nazareth, and is a witness of the touching mystery of Bethlehem.

Oh, that I might share in the devoted respect and love of this glorious saint, so grand because so simple, and so favored above all

peoples in that he was chosen to protect your infancy.

I also adore you in company with the angels, the shepherds, and the Magi; with Simeon, and Anna, and all the church of heaven and earth, which contemplates, in glad amazement, the miracle of your divine majesty. *Amen.*

"The Adoration of the Magi" by Juan de Flandes (circa 1508-1519). Courtesy National Gallery of Art, Washington, D.C.

Chapter 6

EPIPHANY

How striking is the symbol of the star that recurs in all the images of Christmas and Epiphany!

It still gives rise to deep feelings although, as with so many other sacred signs, it risks becoming commonplace because of its commercial overuse.

Restored to its original context, the star we contemplate over the crib also speaks to the mind and heart of the man of the 3rd millennium.

It speaks to secularized man, awakening in him the nostalgia of his condition as pilgrim in search of the truth with a deep desire for the absolute. ...Who does not feel the need for a "star" to guide him on his earthly journey?

Individuals and nations both feel the need. To satisfy the universal yearning for salvation, the Lord himself chose a people to be the guiding star for "all the families of the earth".

*"The Adoration of the Magi" by unknown
Italian artist (circa 1503-1513). Courtesy
National Gallery of Art, Washington, D.C.*

With the Incarnation of his Son, God then expanded his choice to every people, no matter what their race or culture.

Thus the Church came into being, formed of men and women who, united in Christ and guided by the Holy Spirit, press onwards towards the kingdom of the Father and are bearers of a message of salvation intended for all men.

(Blessed John Paul II)
– Jan. 6, 2002

Sundays within the Octave of Christmas Day

O Almighty and Eternal God, direct our actions so they are pleasing to you that in the name of your beloved Son, we may deserve to do many good works. Grant this through our Lord Jesus Christ, your Son, who lives and reigns with you and the Holy Spirit one God, forever and ever. Amen.

Epiphany Prayer

O God, who on this day revealed your only-begotten Son to the Gentiles by the guidance of a star, grant in your mercy, that we who already know you by faith, may be brought to contemplate the beauty of your majesty. Grant this through our Lord Jesus Christ, your Son, who lives and reigns with you and the Holy Spirit, one God, forever and ever. *Amen.*

Another Epiphany Prayer

O God, whose only-begotten Son appeared in substance of our flesh; grant, we ask you that through him whom we have acknowledged as outwardly like us, we may attain an inward renewal; through Jesus Christ our Lord, who lives and reigns with you and the Holy Spirit, one God, forever and ever.

Almighty and everlasting God, who made known the Incarnation of your Word by the testimony of a glorious star, which when the wise men saw, they adored your majesty with gifts; grant that the star of your righteousness may always appear in our hearts, and our treasure consist in giving thanks to you; through Jesus Christ our Lord who lives and reigns with you and the Holy Spirit, one God, forever and ever.

O God, the enlightener of all nations, grant your people perpetual peace; and pour into our hearts that radiant light which you shed into the minds of the wise men; through Jesus Christ our Lord who lives and reigns with you and the Holy Spirit, one God, forever and ever.

We ask you, O Lord, to enlighten your people, and always set their hearts on fire with the brightness of your glory; that they may both unceasingly acknowledge their Savior, and truly apprehend their Lord, who lives and reigns with you and the Holy Spirit, one God, forever and ever.

Almighty and everlasting God, the brightness of faithful souls, who consecrated this day by the first-fruits of the chosen Gentiles; fill the world with your glory, and show yourself by the radiance of your light to the nations that are subject to you; through Jesus Christ our Lord who lives and reigns with you and the Holy Spirit, one God, forever and ever.

We ask you O Lord, mercifully to correct our wanderings, and by the guiding radiance of your compassion bring us to the vision of your truth, through Jesus Christ our Lord who lives and reigns with you and the Holy Spirit, one God, forever and ever.

O God, who through your only-begotten Son Jesus Christ our Lord, has given the regenerating waters with the grace which leads to eternal salvation; and did yourself come upon him by your Spirit, in the descent of the mysterious dove on his head; grant, we ask you, that there may come upon your whole church a blessing which may keep us all continually safe, may always bless all your servants, may direct the course of those who follow you, and open the door of the heavenly kingdom to all who are waiting to enter; through Jesus Christ our Lord who lives and reigns with you and the Holy Spirit, one God, forever and ever.

*"The Adoration of the Magi" by Fra Angelico
and Fra Filippo Lippi (circa 1440–1460).
Courtesy National Gallery of Art, Washington,
D.C.*

O glorious, holy, Almighty God, who being ever concerned about the many wanderings of mankind, guided the Magi, who lived in dark superstition, by the light of a star to your sacred cradle, that you may awaken all who walked in their own errors with the desire of knowing you; awaken us also, we ask you, with a saving love for you, that we who have already known you by your gracious illumination, may be enabled to stay with you forever.

Grant O Almighty God, that we may be able continually to be free of the yoke of servitude and sin, and to appear before your majesty in our heavenly country; through Jesus Christ our Lord who lives and reigns with you and the Holy Spirit, one God, forever and ever. *Amen.*

Novena for the Feast of the Epiphany

(Dec. 28 to Jan. 5)

I salute you O divine heart, with the three Magi who offered their homage to you.

Look on me, I ask you, with the same love and kindness with which you received them, that I may offer with my heart, gold, frankincense and myrrh; that is to say, my intellect, my memory and my will, completely to you, in faith, hope, charity, in thought, word and deed.

Accept my offering, accept my heart, and grant that I may live and die thanking you for the invaluable favor of being called to the true faith.

Therefore, I ask of you, by the joy which filled your heart, when you did see the first of the Gentiles at your feet, to hear my prayer and grant the request I make in this novena. *Amen.*

Finis

Laus Deo et Beate Semper Virgini Marie

References

PHOTOGRAPHS

All the photos were taken either by family members or myself. Many of the pictures came from our visits over the years to historic Catholic churches.

CHAPTER QUOTATIONS

Chapter 1: *"Verses on various occasions"* by Venerable John Henry Cardinal Newman (1896).

Chapter 2: *"Christmas Midnight Mass, Homily of the Holy Father"* by Blessed Pope John Paul II (Dec. 24, 2002).

Chapter 3: *"Christmas Midnight Mass, Homily of the Holy Father"* by Blessed Pope John Paul II (Dec. 24, 2001).

Chapter 4: *"Solemnity of the Nativity of the Lord, Homily of the Holy His Holiness Benedict XVI"* by Pope Benedict XVI (Dec. 25, 2007).

Chapter 5: *"Midnight Mass, Solemnity of the Nativity of the Lord, Homily of the Holy His Holiness Benedict XVI"* by Pope Benedict XVI (Dec. 24, 2011).

Chapter 6: *"Solemnity of the Epiphany of the Lord, Homily of the Holy His Holiness Pope John Paul II"* by Blessed Pope John Paul II (Jan. 6, 2002).

About the Author

MARIE NOËL

Marie Noël is an ordinary person living an ordinary life. Her love of Catholicism, interests in history, and quest to deepen her faith have led her to share this collection of prayers.

Visit her website, Facebook page, or Twitter for information on her latest prayer collections. She regularly posts historic prayers & images there.

www.booksbynoel.com

Facebook, YouTube & Twitter: BooksByNoel

Other Prayer Collections by Marie Noël

www.BooksByNoël.com

Prayers to the Holy Angels

This full-color beautifully illustrated prayerbook features 110 prayers dedicated to angels. Includes prayers to Guardian Angels, Archangels, and the Nine Choirs of Angels for all sorts of occasions – for guidance, protection, family members, and more.

Also included are prayers which an angel taught to children at Fatima and prayers to Our Lady Queen of Angels The rich prayers are accompanied by stunning color images from the Renaissance, which depict the holy angels interacting with people in visions and apparitions. All prayers in the book are compiled from approved Catholic sources. In paperback and eBook.

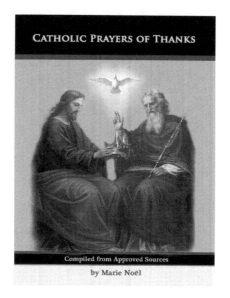

CATHOLIC PRAYERS OF THANKS

Compiled from Approved Sources

by Marie Noël

Catholic Prayers of Thanks

This collection of prayers represents a year's worth of research, dating mostly from the late 1700s through the 1800s, into the Catholic history. The 60+ prayers featured are grouped as prayers of thanks:

• *To God, Jesus Christ, the Holy Spirit, the Trinity, and the Blessed Sacrament;*

• *Regarding the Church sacraments such as Mass and Confession;*

- *For each day and special occasions (your birthday, on becoming a mother, etc.); and*

- *For favors granted.*

It is illustrated with beautiful color photos as well as European religious paintings and drawings from the Renaissance. This collection offers prayers of varying lengths for convenience with the eBook readers.

Catholic Prayers to the King & Queen of Heaven...with prayers for kings & queens on Earth

From as old as the 11th century, the 30 select prayers are historical Catholic prayers to Jesus, Christ the King and to Mary, the Queen of Heaven, along with those to saints who were holy kings and queens.

Many prayers and litanies date back to the earliest days of the Church and were translated from various languages including French and German.

This collection contains many prayers not commonly found elsewhere.

It is illustrated with beautiful color photos as well as European paintings of the saintly kings and queens from the Middle Ages.

Catholic Prayers to Saintly Germanic Kings & Queens

(2nd prayer collection in the series *Catholic Prayers to Saintly Kings & Queens*)

Here are 50 Roman Catholic prayers to 12 Germanic royal saints.

Most prayers are from the Middle Ages and have been translated from French, German & Latin.

Other prayers are to Jesus and Mary as well as for the present-day countries (Germany, Austria, Switzerland, Luxembourg) where these saintly monarchs ruled.

The book is illustrated with beautiful color photos and European religious paintings from the Renaissance.

Paperbacks Available:

- *at bookstores, Amazon, Barnes & Noble*

EBooks Available Everywhere:

- *for Kindle, the Nook, iPad & More*

42788106R00091

Made in the USA
San Bernardino, CA
09 December 2016